Dinosaurs Big and Small

Written by Jonny Webster

macmillan education

Contents

Learning about Dinosaurs

Long ago, dinosaurs lived on Earth.
Today, scientists study the bones
the dinosaurs left behind.
From these bones they learn what
the dinosaurs looked like and how
they lived.
There were many kinds
of dinosaurs.
Some were big.
Some were small.

Dinosaur Tank

Ankylosaurus (*ang-ky-loh-saw-rus*)
looked more like a tank than
an animal.
It had thick **plates** and spikes covering
its body to protect it.
It had a tail like a heavy club.

Ankylosaurus used its tail against dangerous dinosaurs.

Ankylosaurus was very big and heavy. It could not run away from **predators**. Instead, it would swing its large tail in a fight.

Terribly Tall

Brachiosaurus (*brah-kee-o-saw-rus*) was more than twice as tall as a giraffe.

It used its long neck to reach the leaves on tall trees.

It could stretch up to 12 metres tall.

Brachiosaurus and Human Comparison Chart

Big Wings

The biggest of all the flying reptiles was Quetzalcoatlus (*kwet-sal-ko-at-lus*). Its wings were 11 metres from tip to tip, or as long as a bus. Each wing was covered in leathery skin.

Quetzalcoatlus would swoop down and grab its **prey** in its toothless jaws. Some people think Quetzalcoatlus flew over water to catch fish. Other people think it caught small dinosaurs to eat.

Quetzalcoatlus lived in what is now known as North America.

Spiny Giant

Spinosaurus (*spine-o-saw-rus*) was longer than any other meat-eating dinosaur.
It was 18 metres long and six times bigger than an elephant.
People think it ate fish most of the time.

The **spines** of a Spinosaurus were covered in skin.
This made a big sail on its back.
Some people think the sail helped this dinosaur stay cool.

Spinosaurus's head was shaped like a crocodile's head.

The Biggest Dinosaur

The biggest dinosaur of all was the Argentinosaurus (*ar-jen-tin-o-saw-rus*).
It was 37 metres long and weighed more than 100 000 kilograms.
Each Argentinosaurus was as heavy as 1000 people!

Argentinosaurus was not a meat-eating dinosaur.
People think that it used its long neck to reach up into the treetops to eat.

Argentinosaurus holds the record for being the heaviest land animal ever.

A Small Dinosaur

Microraptor (*mike-ro-rap-tor*) was smaller than most dinosaurs.
It was less than 1 metre long.

Microraptor had four wings.
Microraptor used its wings to glide or fly. It had feathers on each arm and each leg.

A microraptor was the same size as a hawk.

Glossary

plates	round, flat layers or scales
predator	an animal that lives by preying on other animals
prey	an animal hunted or caught for food
spines	long sharp points on an animal's body or plant

After Reading

Let's Think About It

- What was the most interesting new fact you learnt about dinosaurs?
- Which was your favourite dinosaur in the book? Why?
- What would you still like to find out? Where might you find this information?

Let's Talk About It

Turn to your partner and discuss your answers.

- The most interesting fact I learnt was ...
- My favourite dinosaur was ... because ...
- I would still like to find out ...
  I might find this information ...

How are your answers the same or different?